AND THEN

A collection of poems

Aaron Daniel

And Then

Published 2016 by Grizzly Paw Press

Copyright © 2016 Mr Aaron M.Daniel

The moral rights of the author have been asserted

ISBN-10: 1526204304

ISBN-13: 978-1526204301

www.instagram.com/aarondanielwrites

www.facebook.com/aarondanielwrites

www.twitter.com/aarondwrites

Cover image illustrated by Beatriz Mutelet ©

www.instagram.com/beatriz_mutelet

For her and Gabriel

—I love you son

Contents

...AND THEN

SOMEDAY

Someday soon
Maybe you and I shall grow into each other...

Sporting a perfect fit.

AND THEN

…and then she said:

"For us, there will be no starry night over the Rhone. I warned you falling in love with me would be a grave mistake. Has your ignorance left you in bliss?"

It was true that her words had fallen upon deaf ears, but in my defence, I looked out for knives, guns, and fists—classic artillery. My efforts to lighten her dark palette with colour she would take amiss. And she was exactly right with what she said about my heart. Perish indeed it did.

PAIN AND LIQUOR

VINEYARDS

When you have been picked, made into wine,
And a gentleman places his lips upon you to take a sip,
Parading you as a trophy in a flute glass,
Will you remember your time in the wild vineyard
Growing beautiful with me?

COLD ROCKS

Second glass...

My lips skirt the rim of the snifter
A single sip, filled with amaretto kisses.
Below the surface hides the maxim
Cold rocks, cut from the glacial mass of dramatics.

Another sip commemorates her style,
how she dressed...

Debonair reminiscences

Sailing beyond coasters
stained from unsober spillages, I arrive,
Dropping anchor at a place
where pain is indigenous.

PERSONALITY

She had much personality.
In fact, many; equally I loved each…
Evidence I am the crazy one maybe…

HOLLOW BONES

Whispers of winter
Her cold frost echoes as approaches my season's lament.

Warmth lacking from you in the present,
Vehemently, I wrap scarves of yesterday around my neck

Only to rediscover the past is too filled with a bitter cold.
Numbness, the impasse cutting at the marrow of my soul.

Still I carry with me these subfuscous traumas,
All that is left of these hollow bones

APERTURE

No light through our aperture,
Left only with *lang syne* memories of what may have been

Our shutter stuck, a future taken in a flash
Snap decisions made through a lack of focus

Left with old photographs, potential undeveloped,
Negatives left in a room burdened with dark

Left with the shards from picture frames,
The remnants of a beautiful image now torn apart.

PIECES

I want to trust you, but I can't
After all the lies you say

I want to forget the pain of past
But my mind won't let it erase

I want to hold you in my arms
Wish away troubles of yesterday

I wish we didn't have to part
But of my heart you have pieces

...and the other half won't let me stay

AFTERLIFE

End in tears it shall, an unspeakable lament
Tragedy unfolds in a symphony unfinished…

Spent, as the end surges toward us, bitterness
Clinging to past, wishing we were at beginnings

Without a balm to ease such wounds…
Resentment, left from all of the things unaddressed

Strangers henceforth, in this lifetime and the next.
Scarred, our love shall not outlive this death

LIQUID COURAGE

Tears leave me. I bleed out…
The haemorrhaging of our love
I spill over, swimming a liquored river to quell the suffering,
Liquid courage, allowing the tide to pull me out until I drown.

Such wretchedness…
a punishment, for living a life I assumed my own,
Making a home inside the heart and soul of another
…and now I am without abode.

CHASER

The line between addiction and liquid lament,
Thin as frayed fibres, of splitting threads,

Drunk intentions fired from the barrel of a shot glass.
Tequila and table lamp, ingredients and instruments

Chaser needed not, nor wanted,
Rested amid a colony of empty bottles

Unmatched, the burn from heartaches of yesterday,
The soul's attempt to drown in an ocean of sorrow.

VERILY

They stood together in their aloneness
Arrived had the days where love had become
a bad habit.

Though there are worse things to be addicted to,
Nothing was worse than the monotony of routine

And soon they grew tired...

Missing the excitement of beginnings,
where love was given verily.

OCCASIONS

My eyes are to heaven but do not look up…
I stare at you from across this room

I extend out from my state, unquiet,
But from this place, you are unreachable.

On occasion you loved me back,
And I would cherish such moments.

Sore throat from countless lullabies
Sung from the soul.

This inflamed heart
Has left my chest swollen.

ABSTINENCE

Acidulous stares, impudent,
From love she is abstinent.
As I ponder upon her fears, we share chronicles of grief,
Goblets filled with gin and anise, poured from a cruet of absinthe,

Quaffs to abet liberations from pain,
Enciphered in oodles of anecdotes
The cacophony between heart and mind, for a while abbreviated,
Wading in spirit shallows for transient escape.

CAT AND MOUSE

They engaged in a delightful game
Of cat and mouse

He would chase,
And she would allow him to get so close,
Before playfully slipping away.

Then he grew his mane…

And couldn't undo the inadvertent damage
He would cause his friend
One day

VINTAGE

Bludgeoned by you to a pulp
Amid your vineyard, my sleeves remain forever deep red,

Stained with the wine of my love.
Though my heart beats outside of me
Still somehow, with unpleasant memories I have learned to live.

Reminisces of a time I poured forth the sweet of me
Intoxicating you with my wealth.

Though from me, many times you have drunk
Now resides a bitterness

My vintage shall be the taste for someone else.

O_2

The man in the mirror stares me back, focus,
We toast to the memory montage at the bottom
of this glass.

Strange quirks as I meander, brevity of pain idle
A cloud of smoke clears amid a
Worthless gasp

Liquor left in follicles of an unshaven beard,
Nicotine on the edges of fingertips

Silence of screams from a soul withering,
Starved, an entire love deprived of oxygen

AND THEN

…and then she said:

"If you think that swimming to the bottom of this cruet will solve your quandary, you are mistaken. There is no haven down there. At best, it is a temporary fix for your worriment. Yes, I can serve you this whiskey, but there is nothing that will burn more than heartache. Know that numbness is not a cure for what you have. First cry, then allow yourself to heal."

DREAMS AND NIGHTMARES

DARK CIRCLES

Dark circles,
The cryptic language of an insomniac,
Sleepless nights are many, and I have lost count…

Still, it is better to stay awake than to drift into an abyss
And dwell in the nightmare…

Eyes open, without your presence,
Allow me to live the illusion I am not already there…

SLEEPING ALONE

Twilight descends upon me
The evening sky, slipping into saccharine memories of you,
Ending months of homesickness and mourning,
Reminiscences of us by the riverbank,
Lips together, locked in embrace

My hands caressing the drumlin of your shapely hips
Pressed against the magnificent moonshine as we share pulse…
Feverish and sweating,
Remembrance of picturesque frames,
The gift of waking to your bewitching face

Clear writings on pages of my soul
Inscribed with wishes to lie in your nakedness once again…
I pine. Heart cries with the tears it bleeds,
Confined to this insomnia.
Without you, I do not sleep.

SOMNAMBULANT

Incessant thoughts of what could have been

Without peace. Still I am haunted
by your deafening screams

Melancholy, somnambulant

The physical attempts to find you
in my dreams.

THE DARK

My friend, I miss you dearly.
Wintertide has divested my flower
of all her petals.

Each summer since you've gone,
I shiver…
Disconsolate in the torrid sun

I fight a battle immersed in futility
An attempt in vain
to keep alive a diminished heart

Even rights without you seem so wrong
I loiter
Continuing aimlessly
in the dark.

TODAY

Today,
I miss you more than most days…

These are the days I crave your presence…
The essence of your ways,
All the love we used to make…

Then the thought is gone.
When suddenly I remember…

Remember all the days,
All the ways you would make my heart ache

PILLOW

A pillow of affection
Softness untamed…

Safe

Dwell with your soul
Naked and unashamed

MOMENTS

Before I wake,
I cling to moments in sleep
For in dreams, we are

MAKEUP AND CIGARETTES

LARCENIST

Lies sat perfectly on the cupid bow of her lips,
As did her MAC colour Crème D'Nude.

Sweet nothings rolled coquettishly off her tongue,
Accomplished archer, striking with arrows of embellished truths

Words danced off her liquored breath
Stroking ego, elocution charming agreeable ears

Drunk from her elixir, anaesthetised.
Painless at the point that she had pierced

With a parting kiss, it was swiftly over.
Her fabric of lies leaving an unforgettable imprint.

After her abscond, the law soon arrived with their questions
Shirt collar and skin exhibit the evidence,

Thwarted in a search for more clues,
Left behind her calling card—this time Ruby Woo.

Revelation that I too had been fooled, duped by a skilled larcenist,
The theft of my most precious jewel

BLUE DRESS

I can still smell your perfume,
The trail you left upon my quilt
Perfect complement to an already sweetened scent.

The smudge of old mascara ensured you left behind your mark,
Mosaics of beautiful regrets

The outline of your berry-coloured lips…
For a brief moment, to the past I reminisce

Of a connection deeply intertwined,
as the threaded patterns
Intricately stitched in your little blue dress

GHOST FACES

Malignant aromas,
Ashes and ashtrays, denim blue,
A tattered box of Virginia Slims…

The puff of smoke from a freedom torch
French inhales and lipstick prints,
Her signature, left on a stick of tobacco

Blowing ghost faces, reviving the dead
Grief cached behind foggy veils of confidence

Consoling her soul…
Silently choking on bitter tastes of past laments

JUXTAPOSE

Her friends accompanied,
Inseparable they were

Scotch and Newports,
Matured slow burners

Long drags and smoke rings
Juxtaposed stood her love and hate for him

Heartache.
With them, she would share the burden

PRIDE

Bask not too long in the shallow waters of the ego
Be proud but let pride not rule…
For pride, she is an unforgiving mistress
…and her payment is high price for fools

POISON

The poison of pride is but a slow death.
It will coruscate through your veins like hemlock
and will have you losing sight of what is important.
You see, love is not to be caged. Yet we would rather
destroy ourselves for worry of speaking first.
Futile attempts to numb the pain in our hearts,
The suicide of the soul.

TOMORROW

If you knew tomorrow was never promised,
Would you permit yourself
to live out foolish pride and tragedy?
Or would you be bold
in all of your decisions...
Do away with all trivialities?

MAJESTY

Incredible ingenuity of the heart
To enable us to forget
Going head to head with the mind's attempt
to cling to poisonous resentment

The heart allows for abandoned principles,
Diving into an abyss in search for pearls of wisdom deep,
Learning to swim against the tide in pride's ocean
Or drown in the swamp of the ego
Without touching the sands of love your soul does seek

Love is not only present on favourable occasion.
'Tis not distracted by empty flattery.
The heart permits actions all void of reason,
Beating in all its majesty

ADVOCATES

Contented...
Lying in the yielding bosom of all your love

Our silence speaks...
Words traced across your skin are the advocates of my heart.

Obsequious, I bow beyond limits
Those worn with the harness of pride

So I will always see truth when I stare at your windows...

All the splendour of you and me

AND THEN

…and then she said:

"A thief I am not. I did not come to steal your heart for ransom. Too long you have practiced the dance of a swashbuckler. So much so, no longer can you tell when you're on guard. An invitation is all I seek. You do not yet know your vulnerability makes you strong. Never with me can it ever make you weak."

FEAR AND ADDICTION

EVOLUTION

Adapt or die

Evolution

Having survived a world of pain for so long,
It seems I have forgotten what it is to love.

Be patient with me.
I will again…

Baby steps

INGENUE

I run from you,
Hoping you will lose the trace of my scent
As if you are hounding me

Though I know better
It seems I cannot escape all the fear surrounding me

Laden with mistrust

Pieces of a heart once broken,
Failing to beat to the same rhythm as before

Antiquated

A task impossible
To restore the love it once outpoured

With all your craft,
Maybe someday you can construct for me one anew
If that should arrive, again I can believe in love

…and all of her ingenue.

PAIN KILLER

Thoughts of you calm anxieties,
Antidepressants, without the abominable sides

The effects of you seen clearly.
See how my dilated pupils smile.

Never dealing with the ills of coming down
Prevarication of my illness, to obtain prescriptions of you

Rejecting all forms of rehab
Committing instead to a lifetime addiction to you

Accepting you in all your forms
Intravenous painkiller flowing through my life's bloodstream

Anaesthetic, lulling me off to sleep
Only to find I'm still addicted to you in all of my dreams

KISS OF LIFE

She would take a double-barrelled shotgun
to my chest and blow holes

And I would die slow deaths
From hot shells of her violent love.

Each time resuscitating me with the kiss of life,
She would relentlessly reload.

I became her target practice,
Addicted to the burn.

AND THEN

…and then she said:

"You're my favourite. Do not concern yourself with my acts of frivolity. This thing between you and me has lasted for more than a lifetime. When everything else falls away, you will be mine. You shall see. The truth does not expire."

AND THEN

…and then:

There was a flutter. A painted lady sat beside my shoulder. Petals for wings, brown and yellow. Warming the cold with summer conversation. Imparting wisdom, sharing her nectar. Trusting me with her fragility. Directions for healing she came to show, and to teach me all the lessons of cause and effect. With that came the tsunami of my soul. The butterfly effect!

BUTTERFLIES

WHISPERS

Whisper to me did a butterfly,
Flutters of sonnets and lullabies under moonshine crescent

…you see, when she is present

Even the sky cannot help but smile…

COCOON

I knew who she was always
Before the wings

…even before the cocoon

ABSTRACT

Love shines truest as the moonshine
Caresses the curvatures of your angelic frame.

The more you glow, the more I am entranced
By the windows to your soul

The melodic narrative dancing off your tongue

Journeyed from the butterflies in your stomach,
Past your heart, all the way up through your throat…

Under the stars, I can now rest easy,
An abstract love made tangible in your mould

FLIT

Musings, butterflies, and honeybees
As they flit beside, pollinating our love
In the midst of a wild garden, we grow faithful and free
Dreams from above, our fertile soil,
Enjoying the saccharine fruits from our seeds,
Sown deep

FIREFLIES

The fire of human souls
Floating in the rayless night
Cast your light, fireflies, fireflies.

Indulge me a guide in the dark, my friends,
My eyes are not enough alone

I wish to walk gently among the kodama
Without disrupting their sleep.

Shimmer.
Illuminate my path fireflies.
Show me the way to peace.

LOVE LANGUAGE

When we touched, she released inhibition
Awakening from her cocoon
Feelings of butterflies in her stomach

A perfect fit…
As if for her existence only
I had been created

She was the scent of two dozen roses
Lilies, orchids and chrysanthemums…
The sonority of pleasure was our anthem

Gratification of deep desires as we danced
Indulgent
Signs of lovemaking, our preferred language

AND THEN

…and then I said:

"I am not interested in communicating with you on a surface level. Or with your social persona. I want to know you, the real you. The parts where our most primal instincts and spirits are in union. Even without words. I want to know all the parts you've been conditioned to forget. Take off your mask, your bravado, this veil you hide behind. I want to know your hopes and dreams, then I will share with you mine. Together, maybe, we can create something authentic and beautiful."

MASKS

HIDE-AND-SEEK

You will not find me with utterances of flattery
Hidden from you I shall be…

Find me with art, books, and music, undone
The spirit's rich expression…

Your heart is more than enormous.
With it, learn to love us both limitlessly.

I SEE YOU

I see you: not yet has a veil been created
able to prohibit

Few are those better days,
where you are happy to show your good side

Styled hair carefully worn to mask your face,
bangs to hide your eyes

My surprise, after all this time,
You still attempt to disguise

Under veils you think you can hide

But I see you…

I recognise the sound of your soul's cries

CONTACT

I desire under your skin.
Remove your bodices,
Uncover you, reveal the silk that is your soul

Let us elevate the impact of our touch
My mission...
To make contact with you whole

LAYERS

You are, with each layer peeled,
More beautiful…

AND THEN

…and then:

A new confidence was born. Removing layers, she emerged from a womb of love, circumscribed by impediments and loss. A catalogue of tragedy, yet within the rawness of her ore, she managed to find herself. Abrogating her adulterated shell, shining brighter than sunrise. Free from her hell, this angel. A precious jewel unearthed.

OCEANS

AND THEN

…and then:

I stood at the bank of a running river, tranquil. Crimson leaves floating on the surface of autumn streams. I would steal glances as she danced among the shade of all the magnolia and cherry blossom trees. Her seasons, every last one, always fell me to my knees.

SEGREGATE

In this cauldron a magic stirs; spellbound
Concurring souls face to face, in the divine artery of the spiritual

We transcend time and all distance…
Our journey to the infinite realm

Without the ocean's waves that sunder us…
We do not fear the mysteries of the abyss

Though seas part our anatomy,
Segregate the touch of our souls they cannot

MUDDY WATERS

I followed her scent to find her wading in muddy waters
All graceful, I embrace her fluidity...
Archetypes of sweet omnipotence...
Floating carelessly on a sedative stream

Experiencing her miracles out on the cape,
Taking in all of her regal beauty...
The sun's silken rays punctuating her countenance
Her colours, rainbow arrayed,

Beats of her eternal pulse, instrumental to a love song
solemnly sung.
Imbuing my soul, I respond with great piety
In surrender,
I give her my heart whole.

SAND CASTLES

Castles, sun kisses, and shorelines…
Left in the sand, the evidence of us

The tide never washes away our art…

All the methods of our leisurely love

SAILING

Say words not with your mouth
Articulate your heart; show me the rhythm of your soul.

If life is to be the game that they proclaim
Let us be king and queen on the checkerboard

The God in us, our sustenance,
Steal me from distraction, with gestures that extinguish doubt

Keep vigil of our love, a language coded...
Together we can sail the eternal distance of our souls

SILENCE

Lying under fall of night, the sky smiles upon us…
Light of crescent moon

Pacific waves begin their journey to crescendo
We silhouettes on the water, swaying in unison

Wearing only our skin; native, unaltered
Rooted deep in the soil of your soul

At the end there is stillness—mockingbirds make not a noise.
Never has a silence been more beautiful

MERMAID

Of fables and fairy tales archaic
All of these from which she is made,
An array of rainbow reefs, coral,
Omnipotence rests at the bed of my mermaid

In I dive with breath abate
Under seas, exhibiting our souls' fluidity,
Inhabitants of the marine, ripples and waves,
Heaven, as I touch your deep

LOVE BELOW

I want to touch the love below
Reminiscent of a kaleidoscopic coral reef
Beautiful, fluid, and picturesque...
Caressing the soft bed of your deep sea

Swimming freely
Becoming one with your ocean,
Our bodies dance an age-old language
of love professed

Our liquidity, more apparent
in slow motion
Both slaves
to the rhythmic strokes abreast

CRIMSON ROBIN

Songs of a crimson-breasted robin
The colour of passion
The bosom of divinity

I feel her breath
Her sonnets
Migrating across the seas

Heaven her habitat
Oh, to be the wind
Brushing imperceptibly against her wings

VOYAGE

Falling for you as waterfalls into rivers
Flowing free and untamed

Creating a protective veil
to the treasures hidden…
All that is intimate

Ours
Wedded to devotion…
Secrets of us in a lovers cave

My Pandora; answers to mysteries of life
Divine
Blessed forever, our sweet voyage

UNRIVALLED

The sunshine resurrects perished memories
My illumine, light to my darkness
At dawn, I am relieved of my ennui.

Flooding back, a warm river of memories
You dancing across the water with grace unrivalled
A manner so courtly

AND THEN

…and then I said:

"If you believe in my word, know that the heart is its ink, and my soul the pen with which its expression is written. I believe your heart holds all the pages of truth, the true place for its inscription."

PAGES

VEHICLES

My words are the vehicles to carry me
into tomorrow.
I am motionless without...

PAUSE

You are all that is beautiful
Waiting to be written into verse,
But you cause a pause in my heart
…leaving me without words

SLEEVE

Your name is threaded through my heart
Displayed unashamedly

Embroidery worn forever,
Just as the stains on these bloodied sleeves

LANGUAGE

If love could speak, she would whisper
A language universal

Directions for all

Understood by the indigenous parts of our souls

CHAPTERS

A story age-old
Let us explore beauty within all the chapters of us

Walk lines of scribes in destiny
Written a time before broken promises and mistrust

An era of faith in fate
A time where love weathered even the fiercest of hurricanes

Though we may lose our page, let us travel to beginnings
Our contents of truth shall always help us to find our way

SCRIBBLES

I am ill at ease in your presence.
You are the sole cause of emotions unparalleled,

Turning my scribes into childish scribbles
Stupefied by a smile so whimsical,

Misplacing all of my aplomb.
My words a concoction of notions incoherent
My heroine, sweetest protagonist
Yielded have I. I bow to your eminence

VERSE

You, my infinite muse…

Each lifetime, there you have been
Weaving yourself into all my words

True and unrehearsed…

Dancing through every verse

AND THEN

…and then:

 With childlike enthusiasm she threw her written note into the wishing well. Faith alone remained the trusted courier of her enveloped words. These, each letter and all her punctuation were the tuppence of her soul. Full of richness, no gold coin thrown—past, future, or present—would ever be as precious.

AND THEN

…and then she said:

"Not every woman is a flower delicate. We all have different temperaments, and each is changeable, depending on a plethora of variables. But if you are attentive, never will you have to second-guess what I desire. Though some days I expose my thorny exterior, the nectar at the centre of my rose bush is always sweet for you."

TREES AND GARDENS

EDEN

No serpent in our Eden garden
Just you and I
Sharing wonders of all the stars
in open skies

Our souls laid bare, nude and free
Each other's temptation
Picking from any apple tree.

No serpent in our Eden garden
Just the divinity of three…

God, you, and me

CONIFER (Forget-Me-Nots)

Forget-me-nots etched in bark, laughter,
wooded anecdotes, the narratives of our hearts…
Scribes existing in trees centuries
but in spirit uncounted…
You make it easy to write our love.

We leave our mark, perpetual ink…
I wish for the forest to know who you are.

Muddy prints of anatomy,
remnants in soil of majesty
Dew on berries
Memories left on needles of the conifer

GLUE

I shall be born inside of your heart,
Live with buoyancy in the depths of your soul

At midnight,
I will have a dozen roses waiting for you in dreams,
Each petal serving a divine purpose.

Though these roses may wither in the cold of winter,
For you, they shall continue to grow anew.

For the root is strong that this love stems from.
I promise always to cultivate the richness of our soil,

Fortify our organic glue

CHERRY BLOSSOMS

You are the muse who breathes life into the ink of my pen
Taking shade under cherry-blossom trees
when it rains,
Protecting the running of all my scribes…
Blanketed by a canopy of cotton-candy leaves

I reemerge only to bask in your pleasant sun-showers
Onto the page all of my words just spill.
When I write you, I never have to think it,
The essence of my soul's instinct
flowing unreservedly through nature's will.

You are the balm to the pain of my love scars…
Soothing bandage to a bleeding heart.
How blessed am I,
A transformation of all my sorrows
Into picturesque pieces of timeless art

PIQUANT

Happiness and her sweet caresses
Invoking in me a fetish for her perfect soul
My armour she was adept at undressing,
The only being who did ever see me whole

Promenading side by side
Together into ambrosial groves of love,
Therein one another's spiritual complements
Growing our trees, lush bearings of fruits piquant

Happiness and her sweet caresses
Invoking in me a fetish for her perfect soul.
My armour she was adept at undressing,
The only being who did ever see me whole

BAOBAB

Do not allow yourself to be asphyxiated with lies.
Breathe freely for your health.
Worry not of unscrupulous betrayal
Unfounded words, and opinions. Others have no bearing on your wealth.

Invest instead in the currency of the soul.
Find value in the process of all time spent.
Embrace the ebb and flow of life's tide.
To even the difficult lessons we must attend.

Do not be a slave to bondage, withering condemnation of others
For in the end, to you it is of no consequence.
Resist temptations to seek savage vengeance.
Enter not into others' recompense of karmic debt.

Do not concern yourself with their ignominy
It will always say more of them than it ever will of you.
For those who matter most
Shall always see your coruscating truth.

So let them posture
Do not fathom for even a moment that you are less.
Your authenticity has longevity.
They are yet to muster that which is your strength.

So do not fall to truncated conjecture.
Stay steadily on your path to inner peace.
Keep grounded as the roots of baobab trees growing heavenward,
A show of your true identity.

AND THEN

…and then I said:

"Worry not about me leaving. If and when I should fall and die here, know that I carry on. As will our love. For you, I shall continue to sing sonnets upon the breeze. If you should choose to journey to our favourite spot in the forest among the trees, through the rustle of apricot leaves, you will always hear me speak. I promise."

AND THEN

…and then I said:

"Death do us part—this can never be. The door of death worries me not. Our love extends far beyond. When it arrives, should I be first to knock, do not mourn. Instead, prepare but do not rush. I will sing about you in the next life, I promise. Everyone shall know your name when you arrive."

LIFE AND DEATH

ABATE

Perpetual tears of my soul linger upon your silken brow,
Anguish on your face. Whence came the day I could not stay?
I thought after dying, I'd see heaven
Only to discover it was here all along in your embrace

A lesson learnt late
In the next life, I shall wait with breath abate

THE WIND AND I

On a discourse with tragedy,
Mass destruction threatens with intent to besiege me.
I, at the eye of a storm,
Grounded firmly in my soil of beliefs

Yet we are old friends, the wind and I,
Though she may howl and scream, in all her clamour.
At our best, we dance jubilantly
Just as the loose autumnal leaves.

Sparrows and starlings join in the ball
Following the whistle of her calmer breeze
Chorale in their tweets
The great owl demands an encore
Endorsed by applause of the swaying trees

So her turbulences I endure.
Death by her I have survived a thousand times
For the same winds that cause all my lament
On the spread of my wings also allow me to fly

DYING

When I die, I shall haunt the enchanted woods.
Long will I have left my unoccupied body to the earth.
I will voyage upon streams of wind alongside cherubs,
Celebrating the joys of my rebirth.

I shall charm generations of tulip trees,
Dance over the brambles with whimsical feet.
An endless absence though it may seem,
Most certainly again we shall one day meet.

So when I die, please do not mourn me
For I have not ventured into some lesser thing
Though you may miss me, do not feel sorrow
My soul had outworn this body…

I shall remain forever lulled into a rapturous dream

RESURRECTION

I use the softest brush to paint you.
Splashes on the picture of perfection, which we create.
Each deliberate stroke suffused with colour and verve,
A masterpiece in accomplished fate.

Since you, my heart bewildered no more.
Your love ignites flames of its beating expression.
I bask in its heat, embracing the burn
For I understand the truth that is our purpose.

I worry not about meeting the end.
The canvas of your soul has resurrected mine, the times I have
died,
A picture unrivalled.
I shall remain immortal

For the essence of your love is life

AND THEN

…and then she said:

"You do not yet know who you are, but I am not
confounded. You see, the truth is I've always known. Our lives
have intertwined in past and shall do so in the next. This love is to
journey the way for us. Each time to heaven a little closer we get."

MUSIC

MESSAGE

...and whilst walking away sweetly,
her hips moved to the pleasing pace of lovers' rock.

The rhythm of her speech upon the wind was reggae.
Her message was hip-hop.

IDENTITY

You can find my identity
in the melodies of my music,

The breath of my vocals, baritone
Laid upon chords,
Bass guitar, ashiko and djembe drums

Its sound is free
Absent-minded…

For its origin is a beating heart

STRUMMING

He listened intently, though her lips were still
Hearing the cries of her soul call out to his.

Her storms were tempered by his gentle doings
Taking time, learning to breathe again through his patience

Shaking the remnants of past treachery,
Losing the trail back to guardedness

Now ready to share her divine instrument,
Consenting to the strumming under her left breast.

C MINOR

You are all of my music,
C minor on my old piano,
Archaic and beautiful.

C69 as I strum the strings on my guitar…

Though I run my fingers through your chords,
my sweet instrument,
It is you who tunefully plays all of me

Forcing the freest expression of my soul…
Even though I only ever knew two notes.

STARDUST (Blue in Green)

Archetypal love, beauty's epitome,
Pillars of thoughts long stood in truth
when I envisage you with me

With clarity I see you,
My reflection…
You colour me the way the sky colours the sea

Blue in green
Sweet mellows of Miles…
Your heart's music
Comme il faut of an angelic queen

Though the stardust of my dreams
I am wide awake…

You
Beautiful testament of divinity

CELLO

Slowly working my bow across her cello, masculinity
Tuning explicitly to divine pitches of her femininity

Master in the craft of new sensations
These principles of pleasure…

Never had two shared such equanimity

VICTUALS

My soul, the eternal pianist,
Plays the chords to augment my heart,

But somewhere along pain's harbour,
I have grown cold and wearisome

The omens propitious not
A love deficit for which I shan't provide the victuals.

I shall instead go hungry
Until all that be left is a manner impersonal

AND THEN

…and then I said:

"Your head rules you, but what does your body think? I can see you writing, yearning. So long you have lived in your mind, you have forgotten what it is to be alive. I dare you to look me in the eye. Your soul and flesh grow impatient, waiting to join us. Exhale now. No longer do you need to hold your breath."

PASSION

ONE

Insatiable magnetism dominates us, acquiescence,
Pride has withdrawn, slipping you and me into submission

Missions of spirit,
Allowing kisses we share to be at their fullest expression

Twin flames…
Burning, melting into one another like candle wax.

We exult in this triumph, love
Souls abandoning our bodies, becoming one

PURPLE

…and a purple raindrop falls upon my skin,
A blessing,
My parched soil greedily absorbing the moistening

Precious jewel, sapphire stone; crystal amethyst
Next to candles lit

Wax dripping
Slowly melting into one another's spirits

…*our first kiss*

GOVERNANCE

The ceremonious burn of scented smoke,
Patchouli impregnates the room.

Candles anointed and lit,
Heat from the raw intensity of our spirits
Not even the sun has known such vehemence.

For the sin we are soon to engage in,
The love we exchange shall be our penance.

Without ambivalence, our flame burns.
Primitive passion providing our only governance.

ENDLESS

First kiss, her saccharine lips,
Coated in angel lust, high, wetness

My hands claiming the drumlin of back crevices and hips,
Gripping, awakenings

Her first touch I dare not forget

A print upon my spirit

…endless

FLANKS

Accomplished in the art of seduction,
To the cynosure of her eyes he had fallen victim

Every inch positively charged,
Vintage sounds play amid the static from the record

Willing, gripping tightly to her flanks
Their essence, thrust into conversation

Exchanges between her womanhood and his mouthpiece,
Swift intoxication from elixirs of a skilful vixen

RIVERBANK

Let us listen to the weather tap-dance gently
against windows.
It is unnecessary to venture outside into rain.

I feel the wetness of your storm right here.
Soon we shall both be without our restraint.

Enjoy the experience of my explorative hands
My discovery—patterned black lace, as I pull aside
your pants

The current of your river increasing
with my attentive motion

Until climax forces you to burst your banks.

CHESS (Game of Thrones)

He declined her frequent advances.
She made it her mission to punish him for his petulance,
Evading temptations in indecent proposals
Staunch in his refusal to scratch her intimate itch

So would commence a purposed battle for power,
Chessboard tactics of a queen in a cerebral game of thrones.
Though a masterpiece of war, her adversary not a pawn,
His majestic poise not easily thrown.

She continued in her pursuit with feline nature,
Marking what she deemed her territory with a scent redolent,
Insistent, as he began to stiffen, provoking him out of his languid
demeanour,
Facing a fight to rebel against his carnal instincts,

Quickening her barrage of calculated attacks.
In retaliation, he would finally draw his sword,
Ending all his sublimation, leaping onto his weapon in suicidal
fashion.
In parting, ultimate pleasure would be her reward.

VISIONS

The background music was fitting
The decadence of scented candles
Burning to Stevie Wonder's visions...

Blinded by passion, opening night,
Enchantments of mellifluous strings
The grand unveiling

Action, unfastening the clasp of her bra,
Hoisting her skirt, spreading herself apart,

Revealing her basic instinct...
Commanding me to take all of her.

CONTROL

Demure, her previous persona,
Until alone. She had him behind closed doors.

His forbearance could hold no longer.
Of his feelings, preparing to reveal his innermost

…relinquishing all control

MON COEUR

French kisses and strawberry pecks

La quintessence de mon amour douce

Drunk with those lips laid upon me,
Such sedulity

Mon coeur

Forever, an ignited flame

SOUL 2 SOUL

A love divine, that is what I seek.

Not just with the intellect of my mind,
but guided too by heart and soul
For they too are smart and bold

A type of love where we are undressed…
But can still have on our clothes…
True in our nakedness

The sweet touch of soul on soul

FATAL

Touching death with spellbound lips,
French kiss from the silver tongue of an adept seductress.

Her artful silence speaking volumes,
Victim to the insidious science of a hypnotist

Bound by the charms of her rune,
Seizing my hands to run slowly over her glyphs,

Defenceless at the hands of her pervasive actions
Preparing for the posthumous, falling forcibly into fatal bliss

SECRETS

Bitterness does not reside with her.
It is absent…

The pulp of all my affections,
Sweet lady…

Fallen, not simply for anatomy,
but for that which is enclosed

Flesh, the mere complements
to her ripened soul…

Nightly, her beauty decorates
my sheets…

Never does she flatter
to deceive

These four walls and the floor
know our deepest secrets

Our ceiling watches on
every night with glee

CANDY FLOSS

She falls on me like the gentlest of rain
Absorbing her into my skin like lotion

Moistening my soul. Rapturous, she arrives
Baring her cup of vintage wine most potent,

Delivering fruity overtones of a full-bodied taste
Drunk, I am of the very notion

That a climax soon approaches without haste
My seraphim, offering all of herself to me in love potions.

Placing a single finger upon my lips to hush
Before administering the sugar rush

Saccharine and lush. I'm high,
Floating on her pink clouds of candy floss

INTIMACY

It's personal, this thing between you and me...
Personal when my lips press gently your inner thigh

Immeasurable our ascendency, enjoying the turbulence
Constantly climbing, more than miles high

For when we touch each other, we touch whole,
More than simple lusts of the physical

Speaking in tongues, an expression in love language
A divine consenting of our very souls

...it's personal

AND THEN

…and then:

There were imprints of hands and feet against the windowpane. Indentations left in the door we had both slipped through. Bodies of truth. Seizing me with all she had. Even her flowing locs had surrounded me. Mathematics divine to divide and multiply at the same time as she pulled me further in. Making one from two.

MOON AND STARS

NEBULAE

To the earth, we look like a binary star,
Orbiting one another,
Dancing our perfect dance

Our light shall penetrate the black holes.
Nothing can penetrate our sphere.

Gazing out onto our constellation
Let them study our love with all their cosmology.

Our divinity is more than light years away,
Eclipsing all of man-made theory…

I lay my hand upon your womb,
The place of your precious ecosphere

Here, someday, a protostar you shall birth,
A divine coalescence of our nebulae.

We will endure all of the rocky phases.
Our love shan't be broken down

Appreciation of one another,
Staying together, creating whole galaxies

SILVER

She sits upon the crescent moon.
Silver
Rich follicles of wisdom full

Affording her my undivided applause.

What is her age if not beautiful?

CHAPTERS (Serengeti)

Her eyes were like diamonds
Sparkling, akin to the onset of stars
against the East African Serengeti

Twilight over waters of ol' Nile.
Goddess, her silken skin confessed
that royalty was her bloodline...

Sun child, her heat ignited my heart,
Falling in submission to a touch sublime

The beginning of an endless story,
Divine chapters of the queen and I

OAKS

In my oaks, we transmute the abstract into tangible,
Divine manifestation, our transcendental dance...

You and I fly in paso doble through all the realms.

Such beauty in our orbit
Universal love at the helm

ANOTHER DAY

Flowers abstain from bloom in your presence
For fear your countenance shall eclipse
all their beauty.
When you are here,
Stars flicker with trepidation...
They have witnessed your soul
sparkle brighter than galaxies

By the explorers, far corners of the world
shall remain unvisited.
To discover treasure such as you would be an
exercise in futility
Hands on the clock waste not the effort to tick
They know you are timeless...
The epitome of all that is infinite.

The sun rises reluctantly, with envy.
It cannot fathom that you burn
more vehemently.
The trees look on in dismay.
They fail to understand
how your roots be deeper than theirs

So when I stare at you
I see the whole of the universe.
Forever with you I wish to stay
So, in my conversations at night,
I pray to God for another day

BLURS

On a starry night, I climb the moors,
Marvelling at the flowers growing beside a rocky cove.
Such beauty do they boast, these hilltops
Close to bewitching sand dunes

I follow the sound of your tune,
Chimes floating upon the wind
The air numbing, yet I embrace the flakes of snow.
Blood courses heavily through my veins,
Ignited by the deft arrow struck from Cupid's bow

I play in plethoric galaxies, nocturnal and childlike,
Enchanted, I dance with the stars
Awakened peacefully from the sleep of a daydream
A panoramic spectacle of Venus and Mars

The view here, not bleak but blissful,
Beholding all the eloquence of your speech,
Whispering pearls to me from the essence of your fabric,
The seam where your soul and humanity meet

Here we wander, no fear of being lost.
The vastness of our jubilance, difficult for some to fathom,
Your virtue titillates my heart.
Our anatomies vibrate rigorously with tantric spasms.

Enveloped in a vacuum of sweet dew and meadows
Nakedness lay o'er
Our shadows and silhouettes, strut a waltz together. We merge
Transcending into kaleidoscopic splendour
Of paradise blurs

MOONSCAPE

You are love's epitome,
Buoyantly dancing with a skill unparalleled,

Intoxicated by the vista of your alluring motion,
Drunk with tremulous passion
of imperishable faith…

When you are here,
An abundance of milk and honey
adorn the landscape…

Eternally grateful
that you should choose to love a maverick,

I stand agape, peering out
onto the beauty
of your Picasso moonscape.

AND THEN

…and then I said:

"You worry for lack of knowing how one assembles a love without instructions, without direction. But you already have your guide. Follow the compass of your soul. It already knows where you should be. It always has."

AND THEN

…and then I said:

"That's what makes you. All of your rondures and lines. All of your bumps and scars, perfect art of imperfections. All of these, every miniscule detail, ensure you will always have my heart's attention. I could recognise every inch of your skin and soul. Even with my eyes closed."

LOVE AND MURALS

HALO

I bet she still wears her halo
Slightly tilted to one side...

It fits her perfectly this way.

IMPRESSIONIST

A long-time junkie for the touch of you, a soul kiss,
Those soft lips awash with promise,

A promise of better days, a taste honest,
Abolishing constrictions of which reality consists.

How I have longed for you, my blessing,
High off the vapours of your scent.

Outside convention, we rise to prominence…
Keep painting me better, my sweet impressionist.

SISTINE CHAPEL

I can still smell you,
Scent reminiscent of sweet roses, magnolia blossoms,
Purple lavender, all infused.

I can still feel the touch of you on my black skin
As if you are still here.
I lie contented in the bosom of your truth

The soothe of textures silken,
The pulsations of your beating heart

Still feel the warmth of your heavy breathing
The shapes we create in erotic art

Thinking of the shadows we left on our ceiling,
Painted like the Sistine Chapel on the canvasses of our hearts.

ASYLUM

Our love is the craziest.
Convention exists not within the asylum of us.

Straitjacket
Paralytic
Debilitating and rehabilitating
Back and forth like the passion of our thrust

Yet we are forever more than lust,
Divine law dictates our vehement connection is a must.

Therefore, I will still be crazy for you
Even when my soul leaves this body to return to stardust.

SURRENDER

...but if it is to be real,
Love needs not shackles.

If one gives his heart,
It is but a choice to surrender.

THE INTERIM

Predominance of divine love,
It never dies…

Even when we believe it gone,
It just lays in wait at the interim,

Feigning dormancy
Waiting to erupt.

FOR HER

Look at her.
Time bows in her presence,

The past and future already irrelevant…
Nothing matters but these moments
They are absolute, everything.

Heaven resides under her skin.
Of otherwise, nothing can convince
A creature divine, 'tis because of this…

I do not question God's existence.

FOUR LETTERS

She dared to reduce all that I feel
To the uniformity of a four-letter word.

But our reciprocity is what, for more than centuries,
Love has aspired to be.

Yet still it is unable to reach us.
We vibrate outside the dogma of all its construct.

'Tis not to be found in a card,
A dozen roses or Belgian chocolates…

So when I tell you I do not love you,
My darling, there is no need to question it.

Never will four letters match our authenticity
Let them keep love…

We are much more than this.

YOKE

Let our truth devour the lies that may fall
from the bitter tongues, blunted swords of others.

Our hearts speak, resembling songs, tweets,
Verses that spill from the beak of a nightingale.

Let us delight forever in one another,
Our mutual consenting,
permitting the eternal dance of the souls...

Abundance rests in your lap
Heaven at the centre of your rondures
Let a love untainted remain our yoke.

BRAILLE

I adored the way wrinkles adorned her,
Chronicles of journey on skin,
Etched in deliberate patterns.

I caressed every scar and bump,
Braille to the blind, nude attire
Petals over my eyelids,
Commensurate with her scent.

UNCHANGED

My confidant,
I shall love you with constancy
Throughout the years and all the grey

Fallen I have for your soul…

This shall remain unchanged.

AND THEN

…and then I said:

"To stare directly at you is to surely be blinded by all that is your beauty. Fortunately, I have known always to use more than two eyes to enable me to truly see. 'Tis because of this, that which is beyond the physical. Those are the reasons why I fall deeper, daily."

AND THEN

…and then she said:

"My ochre, my mahogany gold. Do you
know what all this is, your skin? King, how you
shine. My luminary child of the sun. You are the
very beginning of time, a living map to both future
and past. African. Remember where you are from
and who you are. Warrior Mandinka, hair rich and
cottony. Growing heavenly toward the moon and
stars."

ANCESTRY

LYNCHED

They watched with pervasive mien
As homes burned with wretched flames.

Firemen, police, and white hoods stood in fellowship,
Among others who had journeyed
From far and wide to spectate.

Smirks among the inferno,
Minds so afflicted with hate,

Savagery deafened them to screams
as they pitched their crosses,
Remorselessness, in such blasphemous ways.

Fire in their eyes as they prepared the nooses,
Futile pleas from mahogany children and a spouse.

Spared of humanity,
Their justification—
This was only a Negro house.

FREEDOM

I want to taste freedom,
Bask in all the sweetness of its joy.
I want to swim,
Imbued in the waters of life,
Wide as the Sargasso.

I long to walk in gardens with beds of roses,
To be among the sensation of aromas heavenly.
I wish for nourishment of the soul
For I am long overdue a feed.

I desire chains broken, those that are laden with hate
That I may release this enormous grief,
Haunted by seas that hold beneath
Crimson blood of ancestry

In bondage, they have fractured us,
Enduring the stench upon this inhumane cargo.
Though light peeks through these grated hatchways,
Still I am in darkness.

Here it is wretched
Drifting in and out of consciousness,
Emaciated, appendage to this vessel,
Among those who extricate themselves
From the cause of this hellhole.

I want to taste freedom.
No longer shall I be forced to live on my knees.
I can see my path to freedom
In the beautiful bed
At the bottom of these cold seas.

SKIN

People often talk of climbing out of their skin
But I love mine
Endless like time and full of melanin

Underneath
In my veins
Flows the blood of kings, queens, and slaves

Choosing not to remember for just one month
But every single day

BECAUSE

Why do you stare at me from way over there
With such fear, as if I'm about to attack?
Have I misconstrued,
Or is it because I'm black?

Why do you look at me with such foreign eyes,
As if blind to a human being?
Have you adjudged my skin to be riddled with sin
Because it's rich and full of melanin?

Why do you speak words at me with such vulgarity,
As if I'm myth of nightmares manifest?
Do you feel entitled or superior?
What makes you believe that I am less?

Why do you address me with such sadness,
As if you feel some sense of pity?
Is it misrepresentations on the TV?
Have you been misled,
Misinformed about my history?

Don't you know that I'm from kings, queens, and scholars,
Builders of advanced civilisations?
So when you next stare, be aware of the truth.
I love my skin.
It is more than beautiful.

FOR MARGUERITE

(Miss Angelou)

How will they remember your word,
Your essence...

The heart of a phenomenal woman?

Will they remember all the colour of your ink?
The beauty still in a caged bird?

...and the secret to why she still sings?

MORNING

Is it morning already, my Nubian?
Lying close to you, position of silver spoon,
The night has passed, and my hand runs through your nappy hair…
Your antennae to the universe

You speak verses of poetry.
To your vibration, my soul is attuned.
Smothered in your heat, your light, a reflection on me
A kinship of golden sun and silver moon.

Is it morning already, my Nubian?
My ankh, tree of life, the shape of your womb
In tune with your flow of current
Speaking in magical chants of om.

Is it morning already, my Nubian?
My queen, my heart, mahogany soul,
Awakened in all your fragrance, cocoa,
The familiar smell of home.

I stare at you in admiration.
My soul recognises you are truth.
Rushing off to conquer the world, your pharaoh awaits lovingly…
I hope you hurry back soon.

ALKEBULAN

The headlining act in the theatre of life,
Her breathtaking presence holds heavenly enchantments
A mistress of ceremonies, illuminating the stage,
She is everything, my heritage.

I am high as her essence blows
Echoes bellow in grandstands of coliseum winds
She performs her soliloquy
Colonised minds, blind to her beauty
Strangers to their soul akin.

She is the beginning of my root, Alkebulan,
And I, her Molala tree.
Setting down on me like the blazing sun,
I embrace all of her wondrous heat.

I am drunk, intoxicated by her sweet
Never for her will I renounce my love
She is my movement of feet,
Dancing to the beat of her ashiko and djembe drums.

I find in her my sustenance,
My purpose fortified within her walls.
She is first, never impoverished,
For connection with her makes me rich in all.

She is the very beginning of time.
She is Kush, she is Kemet, and she is Songhai.
She is Swahili,
Ethiopia, she is Bantu.
She is all of us, me and you, you and I.

PAUPER

What price would you pay for a poor man's poetry?
What price would you pay for a pauper's soul?
What price would you pay to hear him tell his story?
That all the silver and gold never made him whole?

ACKNOWLEDGEMENTS

Thank you to God for the gift of life. To my parents, thank you for providing a portal for me to enter into the physical. Know you are both loved. To my son Gabriel, thank you for teaching me how to be a better man; a better human being. You are my light dear son and a gift. I have not known a greater love. Always remember you can achieve anything you focus on. The best answer to adversity is truth. Stay true to yourself always. To my beautiful sisters, Natasha, Melissa and Camilla. I am proud to have you as family. Never afraid to tell me the truth. Thank you for perspective. I love you guys. To Alessandra, thank you for reminding me how to live. Because of you, I have rediscovered the meaning. Without you, I may have never finished this. Your heart knows mine and your soul is pure gold. May the love between us never die.

To my unit, Camille, Kwasi, Trisha, Aidan, Jermaine, Anthony, Charles, Jamz, Leon, Darren, Darius and Vanessa. All we have seen and endured has made us who we are today, and we have seen and endured much. Love you and your families. They are my family too.

Thank you Beatriz Mutelet for the cover design. You are true talent. To Siobhan Curham, thank you for you infinite kindness and guidance. Stay special. Thank you Robert Alleyne for the great shot. Thank you to Niyat, Nat Nye, Anjan Saha, Natalie Munoz, Paul DON Smith, Kass man, Thanyia Moore, Red7Foxy, Justice Lyric, Lizzie Seka, Kevin Langtry, Nairobi Thompson, Stephanie Sexton, Steph Potter, James Chagula, Zoraida Alves, Te1, Babey Boi, Tshovo Soki, Indira, the Gomez family, Uncle P, Albert, Nikai, Jimoh, Farooq, Tupac, Gil Scott Heron, Muhummad Ali, Oprah, Kurt Kobain, Prince, Michael Jackson, Harriet Tubman, Malcom X, MLK, Langston Hughes, Keats, Kahlil Gibran, Rumi and Maya Angelou. Thank you for serving as inspiration, even though you may not have known.

To all those I have not mentioned here, I will get round to it.

Connect with Aaron Daniel at:

www.instagram.com/aarondanielwrites
www.facebook.com/aarondanielwrites
www.twitter.com/aarondwrites